COLLINS AURA GARDEN HANDBOOKS

PELARGONIUMS

PAT WEAVER

COLLINS

D0266680

Products mentioned in this book

Benlate* + 'Activex'	contains	benomyl
'Fumite'Whitefly Smokes	contains	permethrin
'Kerispray'	contains	pirimiphos-methyl
'Picket'	contains	permethrin

Products marked thus 'Sybol' are trade marks of Imperial Chemical Industries plc
Benlate* is a registered trade mark of Du Pont's
Read the label before you buy: use pesticides safely.

Editors Maggie Daykin, Susanne Mitchell
Designer Chris Walker
Picture research Moira McIlroy

First published 1988 by
William Collins Sons & Co Ltd
London · Glasgow · Sydney
Auckland · Toronto · Johannesburg

© Marshall Cavendish Limited 1988

British Library Cataloguing in Publication Data

Weaver, Pat
　　Pelargoniums. —— (Collins Aura garden
　　handbooks).
　　1. Geraniums
　　I. Title
　　635.9'33216　　SB413,G35

　　ISBN 0–00–412381–6

Photoset by Bookworm Typesetting
Printed and bound in Hong Kong by Dai Nippon Printing
Company

Front cover: *Pelargonium* 'Unique'
Back cover: *Pelargonium* 'Dollar Princess'
Both by Pat Brindley

CONTENTS

INTRODUCTION

Pelargoniums have been in cultivation since 1709, when the species *P. zonale* was brought to this country from South Africa. This aroused so much interest that, in 1772, the Royal Botanic Gardens at Kew sent its first appointed plant collector, Francis Masson, to South Africa to bring back other species.

Enthusiasm for collecting new and interesting, even curious forms of pelargonium escalated, reaching a peak about 1870. There was an increasing interest in cultivated plants, particularly if they could be used as pot plants in the home and conservatory. The vogue for more floriferous and compact hybrids stimulated much experimental work by nurserymen specializing in zonal and regal pelargoniums.

Pelargoniums were much sought after by the wealthy owners of mansions, often keen amateur gardeners themselves. Regal pelargoniums were ideal plants for the splendid conservatories in which these gardeners usually cultivated them. First, they were a challenge, requiring winter heating to a standard only the rich could afford. They were also exceptionally colourful and usually massed on tiered staging to create a flamboyant effect. Often, thousands of regal pelargoniums were used. Zonals were also grown, though not to the same extent.

World War I saw the decline of the grand conservatories as part of the inevitable disruption of society at all levels, but particularly because of the nationwide call for economies. Huge conservatories became an expensive anachronism.

Interest did not fade completely however. It was taken up by a different but no less enthusiastic body of people. Local specialist societies were formed by those interested in particular kinds of plant. Pelargoniums attracted a great deal of interest so the British Pelargonium and Geranium Society* was duly formed. The interest is now such that the society issues bulletins about new hybrids, names the new plants and keeps members informed about all matters and current news relating to pelargoniums.

LEFT Regal pelargoniums carry massive trusses of azalea-like flowers in a wide range of red, pink, white and salmon shades.

RIGHT 'Mrs H. Cox' is one of the finest of all the fancy-leaved zonal pelargoniums and it makes an excellent pot plant indoors.

PELARGONIUM CATEGORIES

Pelargoniums are classed as Zonal, Regal, Ivy-leaved, Miniature or Scented Leaved. All are easy to grow in a greenhouse, while many of the zonals and ivy-leaved varieties are hardy enough to stand summer rain and wind. But all pelargoniums are tender in the sense that they cannot be wintered outdoors in cool temperature climates like that of the U.K.

Zonals These are popularly but wrongly called 'geraniums'. While it is true that they belong to the same family as the blue or pink-flowered herbaceous geraniums, there the similarity ends. Zonals are true pelargoniums with a most distinctive characteristic, namely a 'zone' of black, chestnut, red or crimson seen on the penny-round foliage. The flowers of zonal 'geraniums' are too easily recognizable to warrant a detailed description. The flower-head is composed of dozens of florets and is perfectly round. The individual flowers can be single, semi-double or fully double. Zonals are the most popular and best-known of all pelargoniums and are highly rated as pot plants. Fancy-leaved forms are increasingly grown. Many of these have golden foliage, or yellow leaves with a crimson zone. Others have a frilly cream or white margin to the leaf. The most spectacular of all, 'Mrs H. Cox', has about five colours in its leaves as can be seen above.

New F1 hybrids of zonal parentage are becoming increasingly popular. They can be grown from seed to flower the same year and can then be treated exactly as if propagated from cuttings. They are invaluable for bedding outdoors since they can so readily be produced in the large quantities required in such situations. They must, however, be sown very early in the year.

Regals Regal pelargoniums have been favourite greenhouse plants since Victorian times. They carry massive trusses of azalea-like flowers in a very wide range of pink, white, salmon and red colourings. Most have distinctive feathering on their upper petals. In contrast to the round leaves and elongated habit of most zonals, the regals are generally low and bushy. When in full bloom, they make a far greater impact than zonals. They are in full bloom from early to late spring before the zonals start to flower in earnest. Regals need the dry atmosphere provided by a greenhouse, as their extremely beautiful flowers have a delicate surface that is liable to rot if spotted with water. Plants bloom from cuttings that were taken during the previous mid-summer.

ABOVE Most of the regals have distinctive feathering on the upper petals. This one is 'Birthday Girl'.

LEFT Many varieties of regal pelargonium are multicoloured like this pink and white 'May Magic'.

RIGHT Zonals and ivy-leaved varieties are excellent for providing colour in window boxes.

Ivy-leaved Botanically these are *Pelargonium peltatum*, but they are usually known as 'ivy-leaved' after their trailing habit and three-lobed leaves reminiscent of ivy. They are ideal in summer hanging baskets and windowboxes. They can also be used to form a decorative edging to the greenhouse staging. Their flowers, even the most glamorous carmine and rose-pink forms, are tough enough to stand a summer storm. There are both singles and doubles, which last a very long time outdoors. The leaves of most varieties are very tough and leathery, seldom turning yellow as the zonals do. In fact, when their vigorous foliage threatens to rampage over other plants in windowboxes and hanging baskets, they can become an embarrassment.

Scented-leaved Several species are grown for the scent of the foliage rather than for their flowers. People vary in their identification of these scents, but it is generally agreed that some smell of lemons and others of

peppermint. Some are quite pungent, which one may or may not like. But whatever the scent, it derives from volatile oils which are released when a leaf is rubbed in the fingers. It is suggested that scented foliage arose in the wild as a safety measure to deter grazing animals.

The flowers of most scented-leaved pelargoniums are small and insignificant. Two are specially attractive for their foliage. *Pelargonium crispum* is frilly and particularly good-looking in its cream-margined form, 'Variegatum'. The scent is lemony. Also try *P. fragrans* 'Variegatum'. Here the round leaves are frilly and have a pungent scent. Both make excellent background plants in the greenhouse.

Miniatures Specialist nurserymen usually list these under the zonals. They are limited to varieties not exceeding 12cm (5in) in height, with double, single or semi-double flowers. The double flowers are larger than one might expect from the size and stature of the plant. A few miniatures make a pleasant and novel addition to a greenhouse collection and are specially useful where space is limited. Generally speaking, they are not big enough to be effective outdoors or may not be sufficiently weatherproof to withstand summer storms.

Besides these, look out for Angel Pelargoniums. Though not strictly miniature regals, they do bear a distinct resemblance to the mauve, purple and white colourings and habit of growth of the regals. The first angel pelargonium to be introduced was 'Sancho Panza', a pretty plant with maroon and purple flowers and a short, compact habit. All have a certain charm, particularly where small plants are required. They bloom from mid-spring onwards.

CULTIVATION INDOORS

Given the right treatment, pelargoniums are versatile enough to be used as house plants, or outdoors as key plants in patio pots, windowboxes and hanging baskets. They are also invaluable for massing in formal beds. The most glamorous, although often sadly the least hardy, are particular favourites for greenhouse display.

Regal pelargonium 'Grand Slam' is highly popular and an ideal choice for a greenhouse or the show bench. Most gardeners start with this one and usually retain it.

Early spring is the logical start of the pelargonium year. New plants ordered from specialist nurserymen will be arriving. Each pelargonium should have its roots intact and be clearly labelled. The best one can expect is to receive healthy plants of good size with flower buds already forming. Try to pot them up immediately in 10cm (4in) or even 12cm (5in) pots, depending on their size.

If a soilless compost like 'Kericompost' is used, there is no need to crock the pots. These will make full-size plants the first year. Water them well and keep them out of direct sunlight for a few days until they have had time to settle down.

IN THE GREENHOUSE

The cultivation of pelargoniums in the greenhouse is quite different from that outside in the garden. First, the plants are almost certain to be in pots, so they are completely dependent on the gardener for water and nutrients. Temperatures tend to fluctuate widely, cold by night, perhaps even in the summer, then soaring to heat-wave temperatures by day. But good growing methods can solve these problems.

Heating First, heating, which is essentially a winter problem. Here, you have the choice of electricity, natural gas or paraffin. Of these, the

10

simplest to use in a small greenhouse is a paraffin heater. But it does require daily attention to keep it clean, as any fumes may slightly damage your pelargoniums. The main difficulty is having to anticipate a sudden drop in night temperatures and to light up accordingly. An electric fan-heater is ideal but it should be fitted with a thermostat to avoid any waste of expensive fuel. ,

The other way is to heat with natural gas. This is reasonably cheap and can be thermostatically controlled. The carbon dioxide it produces stimulates plant growth somewhat. All heaters, of whatever sort, should be installed by mid-autumn ready for the winter.

A reliable thermometer is essential at all times. The best one is undoubtedly the mercury-filled maximum and minimum type that records the extremes of temperature since it was last set.

Watering Constant care must be taken with watering and fresh rainwater is best since it is free of the chemicals that are added to tap water. Never water potted pelargoniums with cold water. The higher the soil temperature, the warmer the water should be. The amount of water needed will increase in line with temperature as the summer advances. In early to mid-spring, well-grown pelargoniums should be watered well once a week, then left to nearly dry out. This applies particularly to zonals which are happy if left dry for two or three days. Regals require more careful watering as they are coming into bloom at this time and it becomes particularly important that they do not dry out.

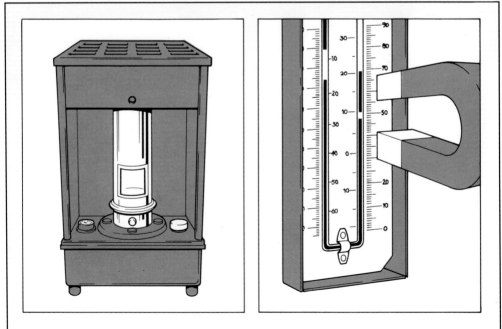

The simplest form of heating in a small greenhouse is the paraffin heater.

This maximum and minimum type of thermometer is easily reset with a magnet.

An automatic trickle watering system, running from the mains supply via a tank with a ballcock valve, dispenses with the need for daily attention to watering.

During the warmer months, from mid-spring to early autumn, all pelargoniums should be watered at least twice a week. It is best to check the dampness of the soil with your finger and decide when watering is needed. Cuttings taken in late summer or early autumn should be watered in when first potted, then left nearly dry in a shady part of the greenhouse. When rooted, water them along with the mature plants.

Where constant daily attention is impossible, why not use capillary matting? Pelargoniums thrive on this. It requires the support of a level, rigid staging and a reservoir of water holding a few days' supply. A more elaborate set-up would use a supply from a small water-tank controlled with a ball-valve. This equipment is available from most garden centres.

Feeding The pelargonium feeding programme should start in early spring. Once every ten days is usually enough to promote well nourished plants. Use a liquid plant feed that contains a balance of nutrients. ICI Liquid Growmore or 'Kerigrow' are excellent but on no account give a stronger dose than recommended.

Propagation Increasing your own plants is one of the keenest pleasures of owning a greenhouse. Pelargoniums come so easily from cuttings that cajoling them to root can be a real joy. (See page 24).

Training plants Growing standard pelargoniums can be a very interesting experiment. Use a strong-growing zonal such as 'King of Denmark', 'Gustav Emich' or 'Caroline Schmidt'; all are ideal for this purpose. Right from the start, when the plant is still only a rooted cutting, remove all lateral growths to encourage the main stem to keep growing as quickly as possible, helped by regular watering and feeding. When it is about 60cm (2ft) high, pinch out the tip to promote a number of young top-growths. Pinch out their tips twice more to produce the 'head' of the standard. From start to flowering, the whole process will take about two years.

A rather similar pattern of training is followed to produce a wall-trained plant. Again, nip out the laterals to encourage the pelargonium's main stem to grow. When it has reached the desired height, cut off the tip of its stem to encourage laterals and the plant will soon start to spread over the wall. Strong-growing ivy-leaved varieties like 'Galilee' are usually very successful grown in this way.

Hygiene Greenhouse hygiene is most important. Wash out all dirty pots before re-using them. Yellowing leaves and dead flower-heads can carry disease and harbour pests, so clear them away promptly. Give the greenhouse a thorough clean in the spring, inside and out, washing it down with a solution of 'Clean-Up' used according to the manufacturer's instructions. Keep the glass clean; this is especially important in spring for plants that have already suffered the dark days of winter.

Be sure to ventilate adequately. Even on winter days, top vents should be slightly open whenever the weather is fit, to provide a movement of air round the plants.

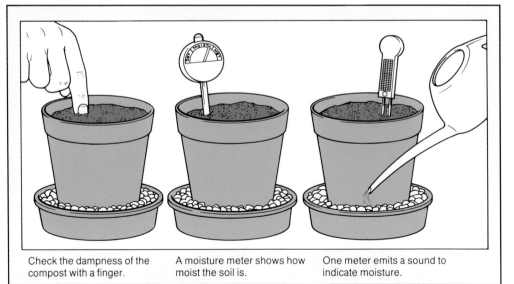

Check the dampness of the compost with a finger.

A moisture meter shows how moist the soil is.

One meter emits a sound to indicate moisture.

AS HOUSE PLANTS

Pelargoniums are highly rated as house plants. With good reason, for they do well in the artificial home environment. What is more, they produce masses of bloom from spring to late summer and keep pretty free from pests.

It is often said that they thrive on neglect, but this cannot be true. The fact is that they show no harmful effects from underwatering for quite a time and will stand over-heating on a hot windowsill. But treated properly, they will surpass themselves as decorative plants and produce a succession of lovely flowers.

A young pelargonium intended for a windowsill should be potted in a 10cm (4in) pot. Use John Innes No 2 or a good soilless compost such as 'Kericompost'. Then water it thoroughly. It is a good idea to stand the pot on a drip-tray to prevent water and soil staining your shelf or sill. A fortnightly feed of 'Kerigrow' in spring and summer will keep your young pelargoniums growing steadily and forming flower buds.

Above all, avoid extremes of heat and light. Never draw curtains over a pelargonium sited on a windowledge on a frosty night, nor on a very hot day. Pelargoniums are tolerant plants but they should not be abused in this way.

LEFT Yellowing leaves indicate that plants are being seriously underwatered. This is critical with regal pelargoniums, which can be seriously retarded.

RIGHT When growing pelargoniums on a windowsill it is a good idea to stand the pots in gravel-filled drip trays.

PEST AND DISEASE CONTROL

All greenhouses are troubled with slight infection at some time or other. Fortunately, there are remedies for the troubles that do occur. Tidying away decaying leaves and flowerheads greatly reduces the risks.

Blackleg The main trouble affecting zonals is blackleg, recognized as soft black rotting tissue at the base of the stem. This is caused by over-wetting in hot sunshine and is more likely to occur in a greenhouse than outdoors. The best remedy is to destroy infected plants and spray the rest with Benlate +'Activex', a systemic fungicide containing benomyl.

Grey mould (Botrytis) Again, look for signs of grey mould on cuttings and even well-grown plants. Over-wetness triggers off the trouble but it can be treated effectively with Benlate + 'Activex'. Remove badly infected foliage and reduce watering.

Whitefly This is the greatest menace to regal pelargoniums. Examine the undersides of the leaves and you may find colonies of them. The first sign is a haze of tiny flies hovering round the plants. Remove badly infected foliage and spray with 'Picket' based on permethrin, which can be used in the garden and the greenhouse. In a greenhouse, whitefly can be controlled by using 'Fumite' Whitefly Smokes.

Caterpillars Less likely than whitefly, but with the doors and windows open during the summer, coasting butterflies could find their way in. Caterpillars betray their presence by the holes they chew in the leaves of zonals and by their black droppings. They can also be controlled by carefully spraying the affected plants with 'Picket' at the first signs of trouble.

Other problems Pelargoniums recently planted outdoors may show a reddening of the leaves, a reaction to very cold nights. They will grow out of this difficulty as summer temperatures rise and the plants get tougher.

Leaves yellowing in the greenhouse suggest there is serious underwatering. This is critical with regals which can often be seriously retarded by such neglect.

Some infections are soil-borne. The best way to avoid them is to use a sterile, standard peat-based compost. 'Kericompost' fulfills all these requirements, and it contains a good balance of plant foods. Use it for cuttings and for potting up full-grown plants. ICI Liquid Growmore is a good general feed which is fast-acting and suitable for all plants, including pelargoniums.

Read the label before you buy: use pesticides safely.

For bedding out, pelargoniums are quite commonly not turned out of the pots they have been grown in, but are sunk in them where they are to bloom. This restrains their roots and in turn promotes the maximum output of flowers during the summer. By mid-autumn the plants will have spent themselves and should be taken up. Some can be set aside to produce cuttings for home propagation.

LEFT Zonal pelargonium 'Frank Headley'. Unfortunately the blooms are not very weather-proof.

RIGHT An unusual but stunning way of growing ivy-leaved pelargoniums.

FAR RIGHT The fancy leaved zonal 'Caroline Schmidt' is ideal for summer bedding.

It is a good idea to give them a feed of ICI Liquid Growmore at regular intervals during the summer – say once every three weeks. This is a fast-acting plant-food suitable for pelargoniums and all other plants in the garden.

In a damp summer, a mould growth called botrytis (see page 15) can develop. The best way to check it is to spray all your pelargoniums with Benlate + 'Activex', a multi-purpose systemic fungicide based on benomyl. It can also be used as a preventive measure before any symptoms of the disease become evident.

Many, though not all, zonals are suitable for outdoor planting. You need to know which of them will stand up to summer rain and wind in an exposed situation. Consult the leading nurserymen's lists for guidance. They usually recommend varieties which are available in the sort of numbers required for bedding. Particularly good are the Irene hybrids which come in every shade of pink from white to deep rose. They make really big well-branched plants well clothed in foliage which masks the soil in large formal schemes. The flowers are large, showy and regularly produced.

All ivy-leaved pelargoniums make excellent bedding plants. To make the best of them take full advantage of their trailing habit by pegging out their stems to cover the ground. Over the season, they make a great deal of foliage and flowers and are generally decorative if the weather stays fine.

On the other hand regal pelargoniums should not be risked outdoors. Their huge trusses of bloom are handsome but only remain in good condition in the shelter of a greenhouse. Besides, their period of bloom, from early to late spring, does not coincide with the early summer to mid-autumn bedding season.

All the pelargoniums used outdoors as bedding plants prefer a light, porous soil. They like dry conditions rather than wet, and a soil that is only just acid (about pH 6.5). Therefore in a typical English summer they should need no watering except in long, hot, dry spells.

Ideas for bedding schemes Generally, bedding with pelargoniums (or 'geraniums' as they are popularly called) can only be effective if a colour scheme has been carefully thought out. The zonals' habit of growth makes them none too easy to team up with petunias and most other summer bedding plants. The secret of success lies in matching the flower colours with each other or working two contrasting colours tastefully together.

In recent years, F1 hybrids grown from seed have greatly increased the number of bedding pelargoniums available. The whole purpose of introducing them was always their use outdoors, with flowers and foliage that weathers the worst summer weather. Never regard them as alternatives to zonals grown from cuttings but as complementary to them. They improve as the season advances and are as tolerant of bad weather as other bedding zonals.

Fancy-leaved pelargoniums like 'Mrs Quilter', 'Mrs H. Cox' and 'Hills of Snow', can be used to good effect in bedding. Work them into a scheme using their leaf-colouring and matching this with the flower of another pelargonium. For instance, 'Chelsea Gem' (with double pink flowers and white-margined green foliage) would be a suitable companion for the lovely pink F1 hybrid 'Appleblossom Orbit'.

Alternatively, choose a red-flowered pelargonium to go with 'Caroline Schmidt' (with semi-double scarlet blooms and white-margined leaves). This last looks very effective underplanted with white alyssum.

'Gustav Emich' (scarlet flowers) would look well planted alongside 'A Happy Thought' with its green and yellow butterfly-marked foliage.

Windowboxes and other containers Pelargoniums are ideal plants for windowboxes, hanging baskets and large patio pots. Again, only use varieties listed by specialist nurserymen as able to withstand some wind and rain. Don't be tempted to put out any of your greenhouse favourites. Their blooms will quickly fall in the first downpour of rain.

Ivy-leaved pelargoniums are a splendid choice for windowboxes. Use two or three – no more or your

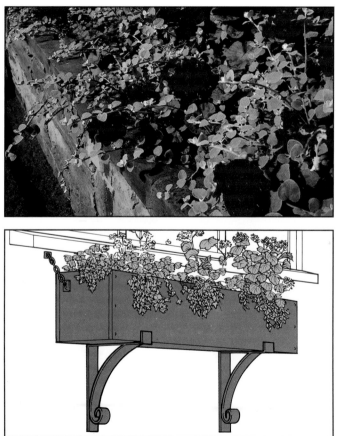

The old zonal 'Paul Crampel' was once widely used for summer bedding. Here it is growing with the grey-leaved *Helichrysum petiolatum*, which makes a superb foil.

Ornamental wrought-iron brackets make ideal supports for window boxes and can be used even if you do not have a suitable windowsill.

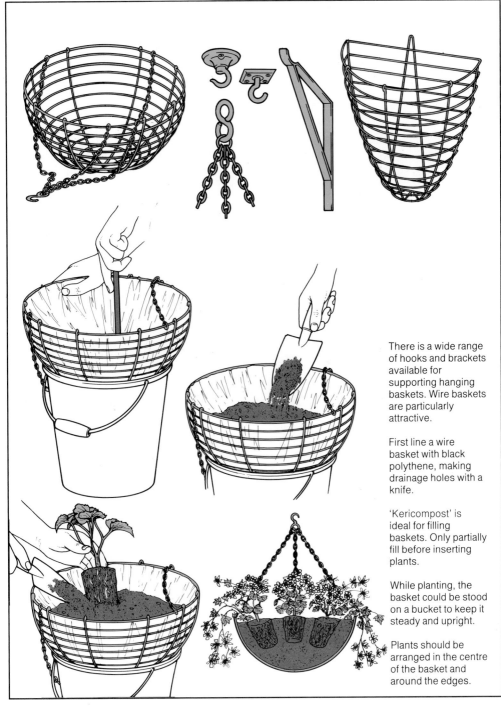

There is a wide range of hooks and brackets available for supporting hanging baskets. Wire baskets are particularly attractive.

First line a wire basket with black polythene, making drainage holes with a knife.

'Kericompost' is ideal for filling baskets. Only partially fill before inserting plants.

While planting, the basket could be stood on a bucket to keep it steady and upright.

Plants should be arranged in the centre of the basket and around the edges.

LEFT Zonal and ivy-leaved pelargoniums in an ornamental container will make a summer-long show.

RIGHT A window box featuring zonals and the ivy-leaved variety 'L' Elegante' with variegated foliage.

FAR RIGHT Modern, shallow, concrete bowls are excellent containers for ivy-leaved pelargoniums and other bedding.

BELOW Lobelia and petunias are favourite bedding plants for combining with zonal pelargoniums.

box will soon be crammed with foliage. Plant them at the front of the box so that their trailing stems can cascade down gracefully. You should get plenty of long-lasting blooms. At the back of the box, plant a couple of zonals to give height to your arrangement. Again, as with bedding-schemes in the open garden, match the flower colours. Why not use two or three shades of pink together, from pale shell to rich carmine? Fill the small spaces between the pelargoniums with white alyssum, lobelia or impatiens.

A hanging basket is much smaller so it deserves careful thought to avoid an overcrowded appearance. Again, start with a couple of ivy-leaved pelargoniums for a cascading

effect. Why not try the new Harlequin hybrids such as pink and white striped 'My Love' and the ever-popular 'Rouletti' with red and white stripes? Reserve the centre of your basket for your favourite zonal. Again, as with your windowbox, fill in the small spaces with suitable small annuals.

Pelargoniums do very well in large containers or patio pots. Stone containers are best as they insulate the plants from overheating. But remember they are heavy to move about. Fibreglass containers, lighter in weight, are a useful alternative.

Choose your compost carefully for all these containers. Garden soil is not suitable as it is sure to contain bacteria and pests that, being trapped in a small body of soil, are bound to attack your plants' roots. 'Keri-compost' a natural peat-based growing medium enriched with essential plant nutrients, is ideal for all containers. All composts will become depleted of plant foods after about six weeks, so you should then start giving regular weekly feeds of ICI Liquid Growmore. This will ensure that you enjoy a good show of blooms right through to the end of the growing season in mid-autumn.

Water all containers regularly, particularly any hanging baskets, which are likely to be sited in full sun. But on no account water copiously in very hot weather while the sun is on the basket. This can so easily set up blackleg, a disease that, once established in a group of pelargoniums, cannot be rectified with a fungicide (see page 15).

Before filling them with compost, do make sure that your windowboxes and all other containers have adequate drainage holes in the bottom. There is no need to crock them if you use soilless compost. Hanging baskets lined with moss drain naturally. But it would be a good idea to buy a basket with a deep drip-tray, which will hold excess water and avoid the need to water every single day.

I must stress one further point. Windowbox supports should be very secure. Immediately after watering, your box will be much heavier. The risk of it falling and causing an accident applies particularly to boxes fixed to upstairs' windowsills. Similarly, the chains supporting a hanging basket must be very strong and firmly anchored. Watch this particularly if your basket hangs over a porch or a public footpath.

THE YEAR'S WORK

January
Rooted cuttings are now ready for potting up in 7.5cm (3in) pots. Water sparingly and keep the young pelargoniums on the sunny side of the greenhouse. Sow F1 hybrid seeds at 20°C (68°F) ready for use in summer bedding outdoors.

February
Temperatures in the greenhouse should be kept not lower than 5°C (41°F). Never allow regals to dry out.

March
In the home and greenhouse, group your young pelargoniums round your spring tulips, narcissi and cyclamen. During the early part of the month, pot up F1 hybrids in 7.5cm (3in) pots. In the greenhouse, spray with 'Picket' or 'Kerispray' against whitefly.

April
Longer days accelerate the growth of rooted cuttings. Vigorous zonals and regals should now be ready to pot up into 12cm (5in) or 15cm (6in) pots. Zonals wintered in the home can now be brought into full light, pruned back and watered.

May
Later in the month, bed out zonals and F1 hybrids. Delay if there is still danger of night frosts. Plant tubs, hanging baskets and windowboxes.

June
High daytime temperatures in the greenhouse increase the need for regular, copious watering. Use capillary matting if watering becomes a problem or when you are away for a while. Plants absorb moisture from it.

LEFT Cuttings of zonal pelargoniums can be taken in August but there is still time to root them in September.

RIGHT The zonal pelargoniums flower all summer and into autumn in a greenhouse.

July

The F1 hybrids should be in full bloom in the garden. They can also be taken indoors and enjoyed as pot plants or used to provide extra flowers in the greenhouse. Regals, at their best in late spring, will be dying back. Take cuttings from them now. Keep the greenhouse moist by hosing the floor and staging.

August

Take cuttings from zonals, ivy-leaved pelargoniums and shrubby species now. Select short, new growths emerging from near the base of strong plants. Keep all plants dead-headed and remove any yellowing leaves. Keep the greenhouse windows and doors open all day to ensure good ventilation.

September

There is still time to take cuttings of all types of pelargonium. Tidy up plants you intend to overwinter to reduce the risk of infecting young cuttings and other flowering plants, such as begonias and fuchsias, in full bloom at this time of year.

Regal pelargoniums are best cut back quite hard after flowering to keep them strong, short and bushy. Use sharp secateurs.

October

Pelargoniums used for bedding displays outdoors will finish blooming about the end of the month. Lift them and rake the ground over tidily. Keep any plants you need for propagating and destroy the rest.

November

The beginning of winter for all pelargoniums. In the greenhouse, try to keep a temperature of no less than 8°C (46°F). Open the door and vents for as long as the sun shines. Remember that the nights will be colder, so some artificial heat is now needed. Young pelargoniums should be growing slowly. Any sign of botrytis indicates that you are overwatering.

December

Stop young plants that are not branching naturally. Keep your eye open for any signs of distress in your plants. Troubles usually arise from too low a temperature or from excessive watering of the plants.

PROPAGATION

It is said that good gardening involves efficient and timely propagation. With pelargoniums, this means renewing your favourite flowering or foliage varieties for further pleasure next year. This is a matter of taking stem cuttings, sowing seeds, or layering where suitable.

From seed Reliable and pleasing results come from rearing seedlings from F1 hybrid seeds. These always come true to colour and type and are as weatherproof as zonals reared from cuttings. Sow the seeds indoors in mid-winter in a peat-based compost such as 'Kericompost' at a temperature of 22°C (72°F). Cover them lightly till seedlings emerge, usually about three weeks later.

When they are large enough to handle, prick out the seedlings 7.5cm (3in) apart in seed trays. Again use 'Kericompost' since this is a natural peat-based growing medium enriched with plant nutrients. Keep the young plants well watered and in a light but not over-sunny place. By early spring the plants should be ready to take, and benefit from, a weak dose of ICI Liquid Growmore.

Pot them up in 10cm (4in) pots for greenhouse decoration or in readiness for being planted out in early summer in bedding schemes.

From cuttings The most popular way to renew existing plants is to take stem cuttings from strong-growing, disease-free plants. Pelargoniums root at any time of the year except early and mid-winter, but the ideal time for zonals, ivy-leaved and scented-leaved types is late summer and early autumn. Mid-summer is right for regals.

The technique is simple. Using a clean, sharp knife, cut the stem just below the fourth leaf down. Trim off the bottom leaves along with the stipules. Avoid using stems with flowers or flower-buds, unless more suitable cuttings are not available. These often fail to 'take', or make second-rate plants. Rooting hormone is not really necessary for pelargoniums but it does guarantee success with cuttings. 'Keriroot' is a very good hormone rooting powder; just damp the very end of the cutting and dip it in the powder.

If you need a fairly large number of cuttings, root them round the rims of 12cm (5in) pots. For a smaller number, root them individually in 10cm (4in) pots. John Innes No 1 or a good soilless compost like 'Kericompost' is equally suitable. It is a good idea to spray both cuttings and soil with a fungicide like Benlate + 'Activex'. Root in a temperature of 18–20°C (60–75°F) and keep the air dry.

Water young plants regularly

Always take cuttings from strong-growing, disease-free plants for best results.

1 Propagate regal pelargoniums only from strong young shoots which are healthy.

2 Make basal cut below a leaf joint and then remove all of the lower leaves.

3 Rooting hormone guarantees success with pelargonium cuttings.

4 Insert cuttings in suitable compost such as a multi-purpose type.

5 Deep seed trays take up less space in the greenhouse than a number of small pots.

6 The newly inserted cuttings should be well watered to settle them in.

and also keep the greenhouse open whenever possible to maintain a buoyant atmosphere. Late summer cuttings should be ready for potting into 12cm (5in) pots by mid-winter.

By layering Propagation by layering is less usual but very effective for sprawling ivy-leaved varieties, scented species and leggy zonal plants. The principle of layering is derived from pelargoniums growing in the wild. One can easily imagine that, seeking to survive amid the luxuriant undergrowth of their native South African habitat, pelargoniums would endeavour to ramble over and round their more vigorous neigh-

bours. In these circumstances they would put down adventitious roots from every leaf joint that touched the ground.

Greenhouse layering imitates this behaviour but in a more concentrated manner. The most efficient way to do it is to peg down any leggy stems in a second pot, making sure one or more leaf joints are in contact with the compost. Water regularly and watch for small plantlets developing at the joints. When these appear, cut the stem each side of the plantlet with a sharp knife. Pot them separately but first spray the plantlets and the mother-stem with a fungicide such as Benlate + 'Activex'.

SIXTY OF THE BEST

It is not easy to say with any certainty which are the best pelargoniums, as personal likes and dislikes dictate what is grown this year or ordered afresh for next summer's flowers. Also, plants perform so differently outdoors, where they have to withstand the rain and the wind, compared with those in a greenhouse.

Adrette

(Zonal F1 Hybrid) Much work has been done in recent years to produce quality zonals in sufficient numbers from seed to provide for large-scale outdoor massed bedding in town parks and other public places. 'Adrette', an F1 hybrid, is a fairly new introduction in this category. It blooms regularly throughout the summer and is also weatherproof to summer wind and rain. The bright scarlet blooms are fully double.

Apple Blossom Orbit

(Zonal F1 Hybrid) This variety can also be grown from seed. Although it can be grown in quantity for bedding, many forms of the Orbit strain are recommended for decorating small greenhouses. The delicate pink and white flowers carry the delightful image of an early summer orchard and should please a great number of pelargonium enthusiasts. The foliage is vigorous and mature plants weather satisfactorily outside.

Apple Blossom Rosebud

(Zonal) The flowers of this zonal are very unusual, reflecting in their cream and pink colouring the picturesque image of the true apple blossom. The blooms are fully double, each rounded flower bud being so packed with florets that these never fully open. A Victorian favourite that is still very popular with gardeners who are looking for something unusual to add to their collection.

'Adrette', a zonal F1 hybrid.

ABOVE F1 zonal 'Apple Blossom Orbit'.   **BELOW 'Beatrix Cottingham'.**

Arizona

(Zonal) A small zonal that blooms at around 30cm (12in) high. 'Arizona' puts forth large, fully double flowers that at first sight seem out of scale with the plant's small size. They are rich carmine and measure 8cm (3in) across. The foliage is a dark green with red stems. The habit is in line with its limited vigour and in perfect scale. A trim greenhouse plant that is particularly useful where space is at a premium.

Beatrix Cottingham

(Ivy-leaved) The glory of this pelargonium lies in its fully double carmine-pink flowers that are borne regularly from early summer to its end. Sadly, they are not weatherproof enough for the plant to be used outdoors. This is one to be stood at the edge of the greenhouse staging and persuaded to trail downwards. It is a good doer in these circumstances.

Blue Spring

(Zonal) Introduced in 1964 from Switzerland, this is an outstandingly attractive hybrid. The foliage is rounded and typically zonal while its habit is sprawling and similar to that of most ivy-leaved forms. The bright clear lilac flowers are fully double and borne freely. This plant will grace any windowbox outdoors if sheltered from rain which will damage its lovely blooms.

The regal 'Carisbrooke'.

F1 zonal 'Bright Eyes'.

Breakaway Salmon

(Zonal F1 Hybrid) The Breakaway strain produces plants with long stems and a trailing habit, a characteristic that suggests using it in hanging baskets and containers. This is the familiar habit of ivy-leaved pelargoniums and it is very likely that these seed-raised plants will equal or even surpass named ivy-leaved varieties propagated from cuttings. Sow in mid-winter.

Bright Eyes

(Zonal F1 Hybrid) The salmon colouring of the flowers and the conspicuous white 'eye' in the centre of each floret make a refreshing break from the tradition of zonals as mainly brilliant scarlet. This F1 hybrid is very popular for windowboxes and in massed bedding outdoors. When fully open, the blooms are held well above the foliage, which is green with little or no zone.

Carisbrooke

(Regal) A pelargonium that is as popular today as when it was first introduced 60 years ago. 'Carisbrooke' bears huge, handsome trusses of pink flowers feathered with crimson. As with all regals, the foliage is shrubby and compact. 'Carisbrooke' makes a large handsome plant that will go on producing blooms from mid-spring till early summer.

Caroline Schmidt

(Zonal) A very fine fancy-leaved pelargonium. Its fire-red flowers are truly double and produced abundantly on well grown plants. The leaves are equally effective, the centres mid-green with bold cream margins. Another attractive feature is that most plants occasionally produce an odd cluster of all-cream leaves, though these never succeed as cuttings. 'Caroline Schmidt' was first grown about 1880 when it soon became popular as a reliable and very decorative pelargonium for the bedding schemes then in fashion. It is still useful today for weather-proof summer colour outdoors. For maximum effect, use it along a narrow border underplanted with the delicately-flowered white alyssum.

Catford Belle

(Miniature/Angel) Classified as a miniature pelargonium, 'Catford Belle' blooms at around 20cm (8in) tall. Its flowers are light mauve with the two upper petals heavily feathered purple. Though on a miniature scale, its habit is typical of a regal, being shrubby with serrated leaf margins. There are several more excellent named forms in this category. Some catalogues list them as angel pelargoniums. They are generally a splendid idea where greenhouse space is limited.

Chelsea Gem

(Zonal) A lovely 'silver-leaved' zonal pelargonium; this term refers to the white margin to the foliage of some zonals. This one bears green leaves margined with white. As with many other zonals that have this sort of leaf-pattern, there is some crinkling of the green zone. This is interesting rather than disfiguring. 'Chelsea Gem' is not sufficiently interesting for its foliage to stand on its own merits when massed outdoors. It is best enjoyed in a greenhouse or on a windowsill in a home conservatory. The fully double flowers are a delightful shade of powder-pink.

Miniature regal 'Catford Belle'.

Contessa Maritza

(Zonal) This is the one to buy if you enjoy large flowers. Each flower is the size of a hydrangea head, fully double and perfectly formed. The colour is warm coral. Blooms are produced regularly on well-shaped, vigorous plants. This variety is a fairly recent introduction and has won prestigious awards in Europe. Having such huge double blooms, it should be grown in the protection of a greenhouse and not outdoors.

'Chelsea Gem', a zonal variety.

The zonal 'Contessa Maritza'.

Crocodile

(Ivy-leaved) The unique feature of this pelargonium is its finely white-veined foliage. This mesh effect is caused by a non-spreading virus and is quite harmless. This curiously interesting plant was introduced to Britain from Australia and clearly marked as 'Crocodile'. Nurserymen seem not to have liked the name, so it is often sold under the pretty name of 'Sussex Lace'. Use it to trail over the edge of low staging in the greenhouse or plant it at the edges of troughs and windowboxes outdoors.

Ivy-leaved 'Crocodile'.

Emma Hossler

(Dwarf Zonal) A variety that has remained popular for many years. As a dwarf pelargonium it seldom exceeds 20cm (8in) in height. Its habit is bushy and the plant of medium vigour. This is an ideal plant for a windowsill in a house or flat or equally for a greenhouse or conservatory. The fully double flowers are a soft pink. These can appear disproportionately large compared with the foliage on a well-grown plant. Altogether a most attractive plant.

Frank Headley

(Zonal) One of the finest fancy-leaved zonals to be bred in recent years. Its leaves are dark green, zoned crimson, but their main attraction is their distinct creamy margins. The single salmon flowers are borne well above the leaves and open freely throughout the summer. Experience has shown that these are not sufficiently weatherproof for the plant to be grown outdoors. It remains an eye-catching pot plant for the home and greenhouse.

Freak of Nature

(Zonal) A pelargonium grown solely for its foliage effect. The core of each leaf of this fancy-leaved zonal is creamy-white, the outer margin green. Inevitably, with this lack of green chlorophyll at the heart of the plant, it is only of moderate vigour and growth is slow. Surprisingly, its single red flowers are larger than one might expect. Its novel foliage and possibly its curious name account for its popularity as an indoor pot plant.

'Freak of Nature' – unusual zonal.

The free-flowering zonal 'Friesdorf'.

Friesdorf
(Zonal) It would be difficult to find a zonal pelargonium that blooms more freely. The single flowers are fire-red and occur regularly all through the summer. Most plants carry as many as 12 flowers at a time. The leaves are small when compared with most zonals, and have a distinctive greenish-black zone. The habit is slight, though this is deceptive, for this plant is very vigorous. Though prolific, the flowers do not stand the wind and rain outdoors.

Galilee
(Ivy-leaved) This is undoubtedly the best ivy-leaved pelargonium for bedding outdoors. This plant has a strong trailing habit and branches repeatedly to cover the ground allocated to it. The flowers are rose-coloured, fully double and of excellent form. They are more weather resistant than most trailing pelargoniums. This is another old plant that has stood the test of time and is no less attractive and useful than when introduced around 1880.

Genie
(Zonal) This splendid variety has been bred from the 'Irene' strain of zonal pelargoniums. A semi-double, this variety bears bright rose blooms each of whose florets shows a distinct white eye. As with others in this strain, the foliage is vigorous and healthy. All Irene hybrids are recommended for their colourfulness in bedding schemes outdoors, containers and windowboxes. Nurserymen are usually able to supply plants in quantity for massed bedding.

Glensherree

(Regal) A most beautiful pelargonium with an eye-catching combination of colours in its flowers. These are rose-pink with a very dramatic crimson blotching and feathering. The habit is short and very compact. Well-grown plants produce a profusion of buds in mid-spring that quickly open. Keep this one on a sunny windowsill and it will bloom its best for you at this stage.

Grand Slam

(Regal) One of the most popular regals to be grown in recent years. Most gardeners start with this one and usually retain it after sampling a number of other highly recommended varieties. A well-grown plant is a bouquet of rich carmine fluted flowers with purple blotchings. Still the ideal choice for a greenhouse or the show bench.

A Happy Thought

(Zonal) A lovely name for a pelargonium described as 'butterfly zoned'. The zoning of this variety is unusual since the heart of the leaf is clear yellow and the broad margin irregularly coloured green. The effect is of a butterfly in flight. 'A Happy Thought' is not showy enough to warrant using it in bedding outdoors. The single flowers are bright red and of a good size.

The beautiful regal 'Glensherree'.

34

Hazel Gypsy

(Regal) This plant has much to recommend it. Its flowers are a clear powder-pink with scarlet blotching on every petal. The habit is low and compact. Both are characteristics that recommend it as a 'must' for the small greenhouse. Bring this one into the house when it comes into flower. But remember that, like all regals, it must never be allowed to get dry.

Highfield Attracta

(Zonal) A huge-flowered variety from a nursery with a high reputation for superb new introductions. The flower-heads are all 12cm (5in) across and so packed with florets that they seldom seem to open to their fullest extent. The colour is a delicate creamy pink, a splendid addition to the host of hot reds and fiery orange tints that most pelargonium lovers have in their collection.

Highfield Fiesta

(Zonal) Introduced by a leading firm of pelargonium specialists as recently as 1979, this zonal is a real beauty that deserves to be in every greenhouse. The flowers are 12cm (5in) across and produced abundantly from late spring onwards. They are pink but with an attractive white eye to each floret. The plant is very vigorous but the flowers are so fully double they will not stand summer rain or wind. Enjoy this one at its best in the greenhouse.

Hills of Snow

(Zonal) A fancy-leaved zonal eminently suitable for use in formal bedding outdoors. The foliage is velvety and smooth, with a narrow but conspicuous creamy margin. There is little or no tendency to 'parasolling', in which the green centre outgrows the margin to produce a

The regal 'Hazel Gypsy'.

'Highfield Attracta', a zonal.

deformed leaf. The foliage is remarkably weatherproof. The double flowers are a delightful rosy pink and complement the foliage perfectly.

Hollywood Star

(Zonal F1 Hybrid) This variety bears conspicuously attractive blooms, their pink rounded shape equals the quality of the best F1 hybrids grown from seed. The flowers finish well above the foliage making the plants excellent for display on windowsills, in conservatories and greenhouses. Outdoors in windowboxes and containers, plant them among bright blue lobelia and white alyssum.

Iceberg

(Zonal) There is room in every greenhouse for a pure white zonal, particularly if it is fully double, of a perfectly round shape and produced in abundance over a long summer season. Such a plant is 'Iceberg'. It is one of the most attractive pelargoniums that can be grown from seed. Young plants can be relied on to branch early, producing well structured plants with plenty of branches and flowering potential.

Irene

(Zonal) The ancestor of the famous strain of 'Irene' pelargoniums. Introduced from America in 1940, genuine 'Irene' plants bear rounded well-zoned foliage and semi-double flowers. Another characteristic is the vigour and large size of the plants. These features have always recommended this pelargonium for bedding and windowboxes outdoors. Still grown widely, the original 'Irene' has rose-red flowers produced in abundance all summer.

King of Denmark

(Zonal) A plentiful crop of semi-double coral-pink flowers is characteristic of this pelargonium. Its foliage is a good green, lightly zoned with crimson. It is used for troughs and containers outdoors and also in the greenhouse for its abundant

Old zonal 'King of Denmark'.

flowering. This is an 'old reliable' introduced into this country about 1880. As with so many of the old varieties, its continued use is evidence of its good looks and its consistent performance.

Kleine Liebling

(Miniature Zonal) This variety is reputed to have originated in Germany over 50 years ago. Some nurserymen sell it under this name, but it is often offered as 'Little Darling', a direct translation of its German name. This is a pelargonium for the connoisseur's greenhouse, interesting rather than showy. The boldly decorative flowers are single and bright pink, the foliage pleasantly margined cream. Its habit is low and attractively bushy.

La France

(Ivy-leaved) The flowers of this pelargonium are large, semi-double and truly lilac. It is a strong grower and the plants develop plenty of trailing stems that can be used to good effect as summer ground cover between half-hardy annuals and F1 zonal pelargoniums. Some suppliers offer it in large quantities, a sure indication of its effectiveness outdoors.

L'Elegante

(Ivy-leaved) An old variety dating from 1870, this remains one of the best ivy-leaved pelargoniums offered today. Its pale pink flowers, flecked with crimson, are at their best in early and mid-summer. After this the foliage becomes the main attraction of this vigorous plant. Every leaf has a creamy white margin. It embodies the ivy image particularly well. Ideal for windowboxes outdoors, where it will clamber up supporting canes, or follow its natural inclination to trail downwards, as it will from garden urns. An attractive pink flushing of the foliage and a plentiful display of flowers can be induced by keeping the plants on the dry side before planting them outdoors.

Ivy-leaved 'La France'.

'L' Elegante', variegated ivy-leaf.

The old zonal 'Maxim Kovaleski'.

Mabel Grey
(Scented-leaved) This pelargonium is grown specifically for its leaves. On well-grown plants, these are large, deeply lobed and velvety to the touch. Rub a leaf between your fingers and it will release a strong but pleasant scent of lemons. 'Mabel Grey' is grown for its foliage and its scent. A good plant will finish well in an 18cm (7in) pot in its second or third year from a cutting. By this time, it will have a woody stem. For really handsome, bushy plants, stop them twice in the first year.

Maxim Kovaleski
(Zonal) A bright salmon-red zonal that does not fade in the summer sun, a quality that recommends it for massed bedding in parks and other public places. This plant was introduced in 1906 and has been popular ever since. It is wise, however, to delay putting this plant outdoors until the end of May as its foliage tends to redden after a few really cold nights.

Mme Crousse
(Ivy-leaved) One of the most popular pink ivy-leaved pelargoniums. A reliable, sturdy plant that is regularly used in bedding schemes. It can also be trained as a wall-plant by nipping out lateral growths as they develop and persuading the growing stem to climb, assisted by trellis or a wire frame. This one has been with us since about 1900. It does well in its very first year in a greenhouse.

Mme Salleron

(Zonal) A variety quite different in habit from all other zonals. The leaves are mainly green with a broad white margin. The green part rapidly outgrows the white, producing a 'parasol' effect in each leaf. Plants seldom exceed 15cm (6in) in height and remain neat and bushy. Mme Salleron has never been known to bloom. It is the perfect summer foliage edging for formal plantings of F1 hybrid pelargoniums or half-hardy annuals such as petunias or Afro-French marigolds.

Mrs H. Cox

(Zonal) Perhaps the finest fancy-leaved zonal. Its leaf colouring is unique: first a central core of apple-green radiating out to crimson, then brick red, and terminating in a distinct broad margin of lemon-yellow. Of medium vigour, 'Mrs H. Cox' is best grown as a special pot plant indoors. Its single flowers are pale-pink and open from early summer onwards but they are insignificant compared with the foliage effect.

Mrs Quilter

(Zonal) There is nothing to beat 'Mrs Quilter' for bedding outdoors. This plant has a dwarf, bushy habit and has been in cultivation about 100 years. It is ideal for any outdoor scheme based on green and crimson, the colours of its foliage. The flowers are pale pink but are insignificant so they can be nipped out to prevent them detracting from the overall effect of the foliage. This is another pelargonium that nurserymen usually offer in suitable quantities for outdoor summer work.

Unusual zonal 'Mme Salleron'.

'Mrs Henry Cox', a fancy zonal.

Orion

(Miniature Zonal) A pelargonium that, despite its miniature stature of less than 20cm (8in), ranks as one of the most interesting for greenhouse work. Its foliage is dark and faintly zoned with crimson. From late spring onwards, well-grown plants will be smothered in double orange-red blooms. There are usually 20 at one time on a plant. A 10cm (4in) pot suits it to perfection. Stop it at an early stage to guarantee a really bushy, prolifically flowering plant.

Pack Star

(Zonal F1 hybrid) As with all F1 hybrids, seeds must be sown in midwinter in heat if plants are to make enough headway to plant out in late spring. The flowers are a vivid red, in perfectly rounded heads. They are highly resistant to summer rain and wind. This zonal is perfect for mass bedding.

F1 hybrid zonal 'Pack Star'.

Pelargonium crispum **'Variegatum' has scented leaves.**

Scented-leaved *Pelargonium quercifolium* **'Royal Oak'.**

Pelargonium crispum 'Variegatum'

(Scented-leaved) This form is grown for its foliage, which smells strongly of lemons, a scent that hangs sweetly on the air if you brush it with your fingers. The foliage is truly curly and stiff. The plant has a distinctive upright habit that suits it particularly for pot work in a greenhouse or as a plant for a sunny windowsill in the home. The tufted foliage is green with a frilly cream margin. Flowers appear singly in early summer.

Pelargonium fragrans 'Variegatum'

(Scented-leaved) A lovely pelargonium that deserves to be in every greenhouse. Its leaves are small, soft and delicately frilly and the whole plant has a spicy scent. Its creamy-pink flowers come in clusters but are insignificant compared with the foliage. A group of *P. fragrans* 'Variegatum' in a 12cm (5in) pot looks eye-catching in the greenhouse.

Pelargonium graveolens

(Scented-leaved) This species has a great deal to recommend it. It is easy to grow from cuttings and produces its single mauve flowers quite freely the first year. The habit of the plant is neat and bushy, its foliage velvety and very pinnate. But its most remarkable feature is the strong scent of roses that fills the air when a leaf is rubbed or pressed. Excellent for a greenhouse or the summer garden.

Pelargonium quercifolium 'Royal Oak'

(Scented-leaved) This plant is curiously interesting rather than good-looking. The foliage is dark green and very pinnate with dark crimson veining. The best variety is 'Royal Oak' which bears single pale pink flowers whose upper petals are blotched crimson. Royal Oak's habit is upright if it is stopped once or twice the first year. It finishes well in an 18cm (7in) pot and is a 'must' for the collector.

Pelargonium tomentosum

(Scented-leaved) Another species grown for its foliage rather than its flowers. It bears pale green, ivy-shaped leaves that are a delight to touch. They are velvety in texture and have a rose scent that is released when they are rubbed. Several other species share this scent characteristic which is often explained as a defence mechanism to protect the plants against grazing animals in their native habitat.

Pink Carnation

(Ivy-leaved) This pelargonium is aptly and imaginatively named. Its glory lies in its fully double flowers that look exactly like bright pink carnations. The petal edges are even serrated like a true carnation. The full roundness of the flowers completes the image. A pelargonium to be enjoyed indoors, in the home or as a speciality plant for the greenhouse and an excellent variety that often appears on the show bench.

Ivy-leaved pelargonium 'Pink Carnation'.

The miniature zonal pelargonium 'Red Black Vesuvius'.

Pink Gay Baby

(Dwarf Ivy-leaved) A splendid pelargonium that is deservedly popular for showing for a brilliant display along the edge of the greenhouse staging. Its flowers are rose-pink with crimson markings on the upper petals. They are fully double and produced abundantly in early and midsummer. Cuttings root readily except between late autumn and late winter. A fairly recent introduction, 'Pink Gay Baby' is a sport of 'Gay Baby' which was found growing in a New South Wales, Australia, garden about 1960.

Pretty Girl

(Zonal) This is one of several hybrids bred from the glamorous 'Rouletti'. Classed generally as Harlequins, their distinctive feature is their white flowers strongly margined and streaked with pink, cerise or mahogany. 'Pretty Girl' is largely zonal yet has no detectable zoning. Its flowers are produced abundantly and are white with scarlet margins and streaking. Like all Harlequins it has a trailing habit and steals the show when displayed in windowboxes, or in the home conservatory.

Red Black Vesuvius

(Miniature) An old favourite that dates back to Victorian times. The interest of this variety lies in its miniature stature – not more than 12cm (5in) high – and the darkness of its leaves. In good specimens these are nearly black and set off the single bright red flowers to perfection. 'Red Black Vesuvius' is one of the most reliable black-leaved miniatures.

Rouletti

(Ivy-leaved) The range of ivy-leaved pelargoniums has been extended in recent years by the introduction of this distinctive novelty. Its key feature is its flowers which are white and totally margined and often streaked with bright red. These are borne profusely from early summer onwards. The plant has a medium habit of growth and it is ideal in windowboxes or as a colourful edging plant in the greenhouse.

Sunrise

(Regal) One of the best regals offered by nurserymen in recent years. It makes a medium-sized plant with large trusses of bloom that almost cover the plant. The flowers are a light salmon colour with a white eye to every flower. The crimson blotching is delicate, nothing like so heavy as in so many other regals. The general impression is of a delicate yet eye-catching plant.

The ivy-leaved 'Rouletti'.

The beautiful salmon regal pelargonium 'Sunrise'.

Zonal F1 hybrid 'Startel'.

Salmon Startel
(Zonal F1 Hybrid) The 'Startel' hybrids were introduced quite recently from Australia. Being F1 hybrids, they are obtainable as seed. The petals are sharply pointed and form a star. The foliage is also pointed with a light crimson zoning. Plants are medium-vigorous and make a lovely addition to the greenhouse. White, crimson, pink and salmon forms are also available. Track them down in catalogues as either 'Startel' or 'Stellar' hybrids.

Sister Theresa
(Zonal) Every greenhouse collection contains at least one double-flowered white pelargonium. 'Sister Theresa' fulfils this requirement perfectly. Its flowers are a pure white with no tendency to 'pink' when they open. They are combined with good but not over-heavy foliage, and a neat, compact habit of growth. 'Sister Theresa' is a splendid plant for display on the show bench.

Tammy
(Zonal) A variety that deserves to be grown more often. Its foliage is pale green and strongly zoned crimson. Its key feature, however, is its orange-red blooms produced with great freedom. Given regular feeds of a liquid fertilizer, plants will flower through the summer and well into the autumn. 'Tammy' blooms at around 20cm (8in) high and so is small enough to be classified as dwarf.

Verona
(Zonal) A fancy-leaved zonal pelargonium that reached us from Canada about the turn of the century. The variation here is that the plant has bright yellow leaves, though they tend to revert to a yellowish-green if the plants are kept in the shade for a time. Plants reared from late summer cuttings should be stopped once, occasionally twice, in early spring the following year to ensure shapely plants by mid-summer. The first flowers appear in late spring. Being pale pink, they complement the golden foliage very nicely. This is an ideal plant for bedding outdoors and is usually available from nurserymen in large quantities.

Vicky Town
(Regal) Brightly coloured flowers picked out with a cool white margin never cease to appeal. This is the attraction of this modern regal hybrid. Apart from this, its flowers are a dramatic light cerise. Individual flowers in the heavy trusses of bloom appear 'frilly', another characteristic that adds to the appeal of 'Vicky Town'. A splendid choice for the greenhouse and for showing.

The picotee flowers of the regal 'Vicky Town'.

White Startel

(Zonal F1 Hybrid) A conspicuously attractive pelargonium in any greenhouse. Perhaps more than the salmon or pink forms of 'Startel', plainly this pure white form most suggests a gleaming star. This is an F1 hybrid that can be reared from seed. Year-old plants can be grown on like any other pelargonium and in their second summer should become large enough to fill 18cm (7in) pots.

Yale

(Ivy-leaved) One of the few really good red ivy-leaved pelargoniums. Lilac and pink forms are much more usual. This one's bold red blooms are produced liberally throughout the summer. Its foliage, as with most other ivy-leaved forms, is dark green, thick and very robust. All are qualities required for resistance to rain and rapid changes in temperature. 'Yale' is ideal for bedding displays in the garden.

'Yale', an ivy-leaved variety.

'White Startel', an F1 hybrid.

INDEX AND ACKNOWLEDGEMENTS

All photographs Pat Brindley except p.6 Harry Smith Horticultural Photographic Collection.

Artwork by Simon Roulstone